KEEP YOUR HEAD UP

Thomastine W. Ureh

An African American Single Mother's Guide To
Establishing and Maintaining a Positive Attitude.

Front cover design by B.J. Graphics
Copyright @ February 1999 by Thomastine W. Ureh
First Edition, First Printing

Printed in the United States of America

ISBN: O- 966944907

DEDICATION

To the two men who inspired this book, Eugene Ifeanyi Ureh for giving me the greatest gift I could have ever hoped for -- our son, Jordan Chima Ureh. To Jordan for letting me remember what's really important in life's journey.

CONTENT

CONTENT (Con't)

ACKNOWLEDGEMENTS

To God be the glory for all he has done.

Mama and Daddy - For the gift of life and the unconditional love and support that they have always given me.

Eugene Ifeanyi Ureh - We have been through the storm and now I'm glad we can see the sunshine.

Ruby Lee Jones - For opening up her heart and her home willingly. Thanks for all the early morning "prayer sessions."

Corlissa Gordon - For her undying emotional and financial support.

Sherry Lynn Kelly - For her friendship, support, and her willing spirit to make "Keep Your Head Up" more than a dream. Thanks for typing girl...love ya!! Now we can go hang!

Wendy A. Evans - For her encouragement and assistance when I needed it most.

Kelly Ann Elizabeth Marie Boland - For stopping her life to give me the vision for the cover.

Matt B.Rees - For his daily motivation through the workout tapes he created for me. "Watch out M.L.here I come!"

Shirley Willey - For realizing my true purpose and being there both emotionally and financially to see it through.

Sharon R. Willey - For always being there with a positive perspective and cutting me up with kindness in regards to this manuscript.

To those P.L.U.S. people in my life that I like to call lifesavers, babysitting specialists and God's angels. The Black family which includes Karen, Charles, Bethany, Jasmin, Christinna and Heather. Ja'niece Allen, Letiqua Bellard Meyers, Liebchen L. Bosley, Talena McDougall. God has placed you all in my life when I needed you most--I will never forget you!

To the financial dream makers who made it possible for me to "Keep My Head Up". My parents, sister Lisa Gordon; Susan Hansen, Ellen Marie, Lizanne Leach and Shirley Willey. Thank you!

A special "shout out" to Qianna M.Norwood and Patricia Adams for listening and assisting me with whatever I needed. Your positive spirit is appreciated.

Makoto Ushihara - For seeing me on the bookshelf in bookstores. Your vision is now a reality.

Ramona Clark- My friend, my financial advisor and my positive motivatior.

Kennikki Helen Jones - "Keep Your Head Up" there is a light at the end of the tunnel.

Rachell A.Williams - For being an excellent role model and book critic. I really did appreciate it.

Tyrone Harris - For putting it all together at the last minute. I owe you dinner, thanks so very much!

Carl Chambers - For reminding me all things are possible.

Thanks to everyone else who one way or another assisted with making this project a reality.

Last but not least, Kathy King - Thank you for all your assistance with the book.

INTRODUCTION

I thought I had it all. A husband who admired my beauty and talents. A career that blossomed faster than I could have ever hoped or prayed. Colleagues and friends who made me feel like I had it "going on." in my life.

But like time...things change. I'm a 35 year old African American woman. I was born with one hand. I've had my share of challenges. I am fortunate to have parents who instilled in me that I can do anything I put my mind to do. I never envisioned being a mother, let alone a single mother.

I had my life mapped out until the year 2000 with what I wanted to accomplish in my career. On June 13, 1994, there was a detour in the journey that I hadn't forecast earlier but just like life, you take what it gives you and make the best of it. I found out that I was pregnant. It wasn't something I was expecting at that particular time!

My marriage dissolved after six years. I must say that my son, Jordan is the best thing that ever happened to me. I believe we have a choice; we can choose to have a positive attitude or a negative attitude in our daily life. A positive attitude doesn't cure everything, but it does help you handle the situation and therefore makes the outcome a positive one.

The most recent statistical abstract of the 1998 U.S. National Data Book states "It is projected that by the year 2000 that the total number of single African American women will be 18,643,000. The most common among these are African American women ages 35-44 being 5,172,000." There are 3,716,000 African American women who reside in single households. Sixty-seven percent of these women will produce children who are single mothers under the age of 18.

After researching these statistics, I felt that there was a need to be addressed, and this is my response.

1
A GIFT

Always remember that your child is a gift from God. Romans 8:28 says, "All things work together for good to them that love the Lord; to them that are called according to His purpose". I believe each of us is put on this earth for a purpose. The child you have could have been planned or unplanned. Pray, don't whine about what's going to be; just find a way that it can work out best for all who are involved.

The fate of your child's life is up to you. Watch what you do and what you say for your child is watching, so be mindful of your actions.

2
BE IN THE MOMENT WITH YOUR CHILD/QUALITY TIME

Have you ever been somewhere...at work, or home but your mind is really somewhere else? Because our society is so fast paced, we usually try to keep up with the pace. I'm asking that you slow down, and breathe out all of the things that you have on your mind. Tie it all up in a knot and breathe in the idea of just being where you are -- your body, mind and spirit.

When I think of quality time, I think of uninterrupted time with my son, Jordan. What activities are we doing and how is he feeling? How can we make the most of the time we spend together? More importantly, how much is he enjoying our activity and what are we learning from each other?

If we stay in the moment and listen to what our children are saying and not saying, they can teach us something.

3
ALL ABOUT YOU

Take time out for yourself. If you pick up one thing from this book, I hope it is to really find time for yourself. We are good at giving everyone else what they need but we tend to leave little or no time for ourselves. Just as we must make doctor appointments, meetings with the boss, car tune ups, car registration, we must take time out for ourselves. If we didn't do these things, there would be retribution or penalty. Why isn't there a penalty when we neglect ourselves?

If you don't take the quality time you need, you can become depleted, tired or evil and bitter because other people are not realizing that you are valuable too.

One thing I have come to realize is that when I spend time alone, I can give more positive energy to others. So in the long run, everyone wins. The question is: What have you done for yourself lately? The answer should be "something special."

4
TAKE A P.M.V. (Positive Mental Vacation) EVERYDAY

The <u>American Heritage Dictionary</u> defines vacation as "A period of time devoted to pleasure, rest or relaxing." The only time we visualize a break from work or family is when we put a great deal of planning for two weeks out of the year. After much preparation, the two weeks of vacation time usually flies by. What I am suggesting is to take a Positive Mental Vacation everyday that includes reflecting on what is positive in your life. It could be at the beginning of the day or at the end. Many times we reflect so quickly on what's not going so well, but if we take the same time and energy to reflect on the positive image, we will begin to view our lives better. For example, I'm blessed to be alive. I have a nice car, a good job, a child who loves me and a great group of friends who have made my life more fulfilling because they are there for me. Yet, every now and then I say, "I want more," or "this could be better," etc. Instead of appreciating and valuing what God gave me, I still look and ask for more. I believe this makes me human. In order to enhance your situation, take a Positive Mental Vacation everyday. Instead of saying I wish I had more, say "I'm thankful for what God has given me."

5.
ADD P.L.U.S. IN YOUR LIFE

It is essential to have Positive Loving Understanding Supporters (P.L.U.S.) in your life. As single mothers, there are times when we are going to need people to give us that positive nudge. When we fall, they are there to lift us up and say, "I believe in you — keep the faith." Those P.L.U.S. people are also there to share in our successes and failures and love us unconditionally. I believe a positive attitude is contagious.

To become a Positive Loving Understanding Supporter, here are some steps to assist you:

1. Say encouraging words.
2. Be non-judgmental of decisions made.
3. Have a "Can Do" answer toward questions. For example, do you think you could go back to school to better yourself? A P.L.U.S. person's response is "The sky is the limit" and "I can do anything I put my mind to doing."
4. Recognize small to large success examples – Stay positive throughout the day while managing you and your child's life.

Take the P.L.U.S. test: Are people running away from you or towards you?

Positive Loving Understanding Supporters add to the quality of your life. Always run to these people and practice being a Positive Loving Understanding Supporter yourself.

6
RUN AT AN EXCEPTIONAL RATE TO AVOID NEGATIVE ANNOYING GLOOMY SUPPORTERS (N.A.G.S.).

When thinking about this strategy, I was trying to decide why I didn't say eliminate or limit the interaction. Most times these people are family members, friends and co-workers.

What constitutes a person being a Negative Annoying Gloomy Supporter (N.A.G.S.)? Here are some of the phrases they often use:

1. "This will never work."
2. "I told you he wasn't any good."
3. "You look fat in that dress."
4. "If you would have listened to me in the first place, this would have never happened!"
5. "What's the point of trying? You are going to fall flat on your face anyway."
6. "Your life couldn't get any worse!"
7. "I've always done it this way so why change?"

Do any of these phrases sound familiar? If so, you have just encountered a N.A.G.S. like behavior. I am fortunate to have a lot of N.A.G.S. in my life; I try to encourage them to become a P.L.U.S. instead of N.A.G.S. When I am unsuccessful in this endeavor, I usually try to avoid them. Just like positive attitudes are contagious, so are negative ones.

It's amazing how easily someone can point out the negative and just bypass all of the positive. But it takes a little bit more energy and kindness to see the good in the person you are supporting. The one thing that the P.L.U.S. and N.A.G.S. have in common is that they love you. But, express it differently.

7
IF YOU MUST HAVE A "PITY PARTY", ONLY INVITE THE P.L.U.S. PEOPLE.

There are going to be valleys in your life. Iyanla Vanzant, author of Faith in the Valley, describes valleys as "Those tight spots, dark places, uncomfortable situations we think make our lives so miserable." When we are at these points in our life, we start feeling sorry for ourselves. "I should have done it better." "How could I be so stupid!" Does any of this sound familiar?

I believe it's good to have a "pity party" but only if we limit the time and the people we invite. After we have acknowledged why our life is so miserable, usually a P.L.U.S. will say "But look how well you are raising your son." "This, too, shall pass." "This won't go on forever." "Keep your head up." "There is a light at the end of the tunnel." Be very aware of those uninvited N.A.G.S. who feel they must attend despite all your protest.

Write down five things you could do immediately to get out of your slump and put your positive thoughts into action. Valleys will come in our lives. It's how we handle those situations when opportunities arise that enrich our lives.

8
THERE ARE 1440 MINUTES IN A DAY, IMAGINE THE ENDLESS POSSIBILITIES

There is never enough time to do what you want to do. Have you really broken it down minute by the minute? Imagine where all your times goes. I'm a visual person, so here's a day in my life on a weekday.

1. Sleep six hours a day – 360 minutes
2. Work for 10 hours (including the commute) – 600 minutes
3. Exercise for one hour and shower – 90 minutes
4. Get Jordan dressed and connect with him in the morning – 60 minutes
5. Prepare and eat dinner and take a P.M.V. while Jordan is playing with his toys – 45 minutes
6. Read for inspiration and encouragement, or just romance novels – 60 to 90 minutes according to how engrossing the subject is at hand.
7. Give Jordan a bath at bedtime and read – 60 minutes.

There are 120 minutes unaccounted for but let me assure you that they are very well spent! There will be those unexpected things that will creep into your life and take your time but if you prioritize, plan and pray, the execution of your day will go smoother than you anticipated.

9
ROMANCE FOR THE SINGLE MOTHER

There are many demands on our time already. How is it possible to also date? "All things worth having are worth taking a chance on." My life presently is full and I'm not eager to jump back out on the dating scene. However, that's a conscious choice I have made. I am still working to complete me, because so many times we feel a partner should complete us. I believe we should feel complete and a partner should complement who we already are in life.

I suggest the following questions to ask when looking for the right man:

1. Does he love children?
2. Is he willing to accept your child or family?
3. Are you lonely or are you really interested?

Don't expose your child to him until you're sure he's semi-serious about you and your child. Don't settle for just anyone. Have a vision of what you want, and hopefully that dream will become a reality. I have noticed good things come to us when we are not expecting or looking for them, and I think that's true for the single mother and romance.

10
QUIET TIME WITH GOD

There is something to be said for quiet, quality time with yourself. Now imagine quiet time with God. I describe this as a one-on-one between God and you. No one else can disturb or interrupt. In this time together when you are thanking Him for how good He has been. He has been better to you than you have been to yourself. He has made a way out of no way.

I read the Bible to get a better understanding of His word. I find it energizing and refreshing. I talk to God about my aspirations, hopes, and fears. Our prayers will be answered. All we have to do is take the time to connect with God. It is worth the time. Often, the only time we connect with God is when things are not going well in our lives. Imagine if we connected with God on a regular basis how much better we would feel mentally, emotionally and spiritually.

11
REMEMBER TO S.E.E.
(Self Esteem Enhancers) THE GOOD

This strategy is one of the most exciting for me. If you pick up any suggestion that will encourage you to be all you can be, then I feel I've made a small difference in your life.

I define Self Esteem Enhancers as anything that will make you feel good about yourself on the inside. Here are a few suggestions for inner strength:

1. Exercise at least three times a week. It will give you vitality and energy.
2. You are what you eat. Watch what you put into our body.
3. Create an "Admiration List" by writing down five qualities you admire about yourself. Here are five qualities that I possess.

    a. Positive attitude
    b. Good listener
    c. Good mother
    d. Motivator
    e. Self starter

Post these qualities where you can see them everyday. Create an admiration list of your own and update it every two weeks. It's important to pump yourself up! So many times we wait for others to encourage us. When that's not available,we have the power within ourselves to be our own motivator.

4. Bi-weekly or monthly trip to the hair stylist
5. Bi-weekly or monthly manicure and pedicure

As you enhance yourself on the inside, it's essential that your outside reflect how good you feel.

6. Knowledge is power. We feel more intelligent as we continue to expose ourselves to new and different things. This also enhances our ability to S.E.E. the good. Others will recognize you and want to know your secrets.

12
FIT EXERCISE INTO YOUR LIFESTYLE

It is very interesting to me that we (my sister friends) can do everything – juggle a job, children, manage a household, attend PTA meetings, hang out with friends and even manage to get involved with committees at church. However, when it's time to take care of themselves by exercising they say, "We're too busy." I challenge you to fit it in. I believe we as African American women, tend to neglect our temples (bodies) until something happens. For example, if we go to the doctor he/she says we have high blood pressure or high cholesterol, we're in danger of heart problems or diabetes, etc. if we don't take care of our bodies.

When I speak of exercising, I think of it as something I can fit in my day which will make everything better. If you've never exercised before or if it has been a while, start off SLOW. You may want to start by walking 15 minutes four times a week and gradually increase by five minute increments every week until you are up to 30 minutes at least three times a week.

Here's a challenge: if you don't feel better, more empowered, energetic, vitalized and refreshed for having exercised, **I will refund your money from this book.** I'm very serious about this challenge!

My final thought on this is "Just Do It". Stop making excuses!!!

13
LEAD BY EXAMPLE

So many times we wonder how did our children get the way they are? They are a product of their environment. It's amazing to me how children pick up everything including the things that we don't want them to inherit! There's a simple solution to this problem: Talk the talk and walk the walk. Say what you mean and mean what you say. If you tell your child to watch his/her profanity or attitude, watch yourself as well! My mother always says "The fruit doesn't fall far from the tree." In other words, your child picks up many of his/her behaviors from YOU.

14
TWO-WAY MIRROR

How you see yourself in the mirror and how you feel about yourself (self-esteem) are two pictures that can look very different. I heard a story the other day that fits well here. A Pike fish, who normally eats Mineral fish, was in an aquarium with a Mineral fish There was a glass wall separating them for six weeks, every time the Pike fish tried to eat the Mineral fish, they would hit their heads on the glass wall. The glass wall was removed and the Mineral fish came closer to the Pike fish but they would do nothing. They had developed an image of themselves getting hit by the glass wall. When the glass was taken away, it didn't make any difference that the image was false because it was real to the Pike fish.

Julia Boyd, author, stated "In the company of my sisters, Black women and self-esteem to develop and maintain a healthy sense of self- esteem, we need to receive two basic messages: I am lovable and I am worthwhile." We need to get these messages consistently. She goes on to write "It takes three things to turn a message into a belief." They are as follows:

1. The message must be given in a clear and direct manner.
2. There has to be supportive evidence that increases the validity of the message.
3. The message must be repeated over an extended period of time.

Whatever you see in the mirror, you have the power to make a positive change if that is your desire. Don't continue to accept the picture and be hurt, angry or bitter, recognize that the glass wall is no longer there and cross over to a new you. I know that this is much easier said than done, but I urge you to be more intentional about changing and improving your self-esteem.

Here are some suggestions:

1. If you think you are overweight and that's "weighing you down" – ask yourself, what can I do to change my image? (Lose weight)
2. If you have a negative attitude and it's hard for you to keep friends, (refer to the P.L.U.S. strategy in this book), Strategy 5.
3. If you rely on others to pump you up then you give others too much power. For example, if you ask "Do you like this outfit, this boyfriend, this car?"- you are setting yourself up for disappointment. If others don't like the choices you've made, simply rephrase the question by saying "What is your opinion of......". Everyone is entitled to his/her opinion. If you want an opinion, ask a P.L.U.S. person who will give an honest answer. Don't ask a N.A.G.S. P.L.U.S.' will tell you the truth with more diplomacy. Ask what do you want to see in your two way mirror? By utilizing your power from within, you can create a more positive image.

15
BELIEVE YOU CAN FLY
(NOURISH YOUR DREAM)

There are so many things to believe in. My challenge to you is to believe in yourself. There are things you want to accomplish in your life but if you are afraid of taking those risks, you will never get to the next level. Sure, there are some risks where you may fall flat on your face, but there are others risks where you can fly. I especially like the song by R. Kelly – "I Believe I Can Fly". If you don't have faith in yourself, it's really difficult for others to believe in you.

A good example is that plants, must be nourished with water or they will die. We are very similar in that way. If we don't nourish our dreams, they will die. Have you ever noticed that some people are always excelling and you think-- what are they doing that I'm not? They have an action plan for making their dreams come true. Here are some examples of action plans:

1. Set short term (1-year) and long term (3-5 years) goals. Short term goals are crucial to completing your long term goals. I am the type of person who must see results immediately. By doing so, I know I'm on the right track and nourishing my dream. An example of this is: I have a goal to lose weight within a certain length of time. Now this is definitely a long term goal. But my short term goals are to walk 40 minutes, four times a week; eat healthy; cut out fast food (believe me, this is no easy feat); and weigh myself every Sunday. Now I must say that on the weeks when pounds come off I am happy. However, on the weeks that I gained or remained the same when adhering to my "Lifestyle Plan," I feel discouraged so I play different word games to enhance my success. I start measuring success by how loose my clothes fit and how many inches I've lost.

2. Write down your dreams and thoughts of how you are feeling while going through this journey in a journal. You can always look back on it and reflect.

3. Add those P.L.U.S. in your plan for encouragement.

"Believe You Can Fly" and nourish your dream. It's not enough to say what you intend to do. Have a plan of which dreams are the most real for you and how you can make each dream a reality or "fly". There are going to be days you can barely fly and you will fall, and that's okay. To that I say get up, brush yourself off and try again.

16
SHIFT YOUR WAY OF THINKING

When I was about 13 years old, I remember a television commercial that said "It takes two hands to handle a Whopper at Burger King". Well, the average person might not be phased by this, but I was born without my lower right arm. Before this commercial I had no problem eating a Whopper. Now I had to think, "Did I really need two hands to eat a Whopper?" Sorry, but the answer was and is NO! But if I didn't know any better or hadn't eaten a Whopper before this TV commercial, I probably would have believed this ad.

Sometimes we have to shift our way of thinking. In jobs or family situations, we may feel stifled or inhibited. It is difficult to find the positive. The common response may be it's always been this way and it will never change.

Shift your way of thinking about situations by asking yourself this question, How can this situation work for me?

When you take the time to question your present condition, you are ready for some positive change. It won't be easy, but anything in your life worth having isn't. The payoff in the long run is very worthwhile.

17
SMILE IT INCREASES YOUR FACE VALUE

This strategy.is the easiest to do, but the hardest for some of my sister friends. It is said that it takes 72 muscles to frown and only 14 to smile. One of my friends would tease me and say look at how many calories I'm burning by not smiling. I, in turn, would laugh and say, "But look at what other people are missing." There are so many things in this life that are expensive to give away. It costs you nothing to smile at another sister friend, yet it is not done often enough.

Next week, intentionally smile at 10 people you meet. Watch their response and notice how much better you feel. I challenge you to ask yourself these questions:

1. What is it about my life that is making me so unhappy that I can't give a smile away?
2. How can I become a more positive person?

Think about those people whom you admire. How friendly are they? Do they have high self-esteem? Are they happy with themselves? What's inside your heart that expresses your actions. One of my favorite phrases is "Your body is speaking so loudly that I can't hear what you are saying." I believe we could reach more sister friends if we would be nicer to each other. Take action immediately; give a smile away today.

18
LIGHTEN UP – SEE THE G.L.O.W.

We have so much on our plates, that we are often tense, anxious or nervous because something can't get paid or we can't satisfy someone in our world. It's not going to get better unless we just relax.

Lighten up – Let It G. (God's) L. (Lights provides) O. (Opportunity for a) W. (Winning Attitude)! Life will go more smoothly if we let it G.L.O.W. So many times we try to do everything by ourselves. Ask God for guidance and understanding, and He will direct your path.

You might say you're too busy to lighten up. But let me caution you to take a moment to see how you react to a situation that didn't go smoothly. If only you would have lightened up, your stress would be less. There are some things you can prevent if you are proactive. A couple of suggestions that I find very helpful are:

1. Take 10 deep breaths, blowing out the negative energy and inhaling the positive.
2. Roll your shoulders back and forth and turn your head to one side. Then roll your head to the front, then to the other side and then to the back. Repeat this a couple of times and feel your body relaxing. You will enjoy life more if you're not taking everything so seriously.

19
IF POSSIBLE, CREATE, ESTABLISH AND
NOURISH YOUR RELATIONSHIP WITH
THE CHILD'S FATHER

I want to acknowledge that depending on different situations, this may not be possible. But if it is possible, establishing a positive relationship with your child's father -- "Do It Now!"

I was at an awards banquet for Benjamin E. Mays Academy. Dr. James C. Perkins, founder and director of the school, said "A child can't be what they can't see." If children don't see their father or positive Black role models as doctors, lawyers, teachers or good fathers, how can that child grow up to be what he/she hasn't experienced or seen?

As mothers we give our child everything he/she desires but we cannot be fathers. Here are a few suggestions for making the father of your child a positive influence:

1. Let your child spend time alone with his/her father.
2. Talk positive about their father or if you don't have anything good to say, say nothing.
3. Keep in touch and tell him about your child's progress.

The relationship may have dissolved, but your child shouldn't suffer. This is easier said than done. When I knew my marriage wasn't going to last, I wanted to end it before I started resenting him or became bitter. So for the first two months of Jordan's life, I avoided him because I was very angry, and I needed to work through it.

Do whatever you need to do to jump over that obstacle. Talk to a counselor, a preacher or a friend; but master that hurdle because your child is the one who will be heavily impacted. People say, "Well at least he's paying child support." To that I say it's not just the money, it's about being present for your child. If his/her father is not present, a mentor or a Big Brother/Sister is encouraged.

20
SHOW ME SOME LOVE

At least three times everyday I will say to Jordan, "Show me some love," which means give me a hug. I do this before leaving in the morning and before bedtime. I now see him spontaneously hugging family members. I look at him and think if we could be like a child and give hugs away so freely and uninhibited, how much better we would feel about ourselves and life's journey here on earth.

It has been said that hug makes you smile, relieve tension and make you feel valued and loved. So why is it that we are stingy when giving them out? When was the last time you showed some love to your child? Hugs are free and will make him/her feel special, appreciated and above all, <u>loved</u>.

21
SLOW DOWN

We are always so busy that we don't take the time to slow down. I've found that sometimes God will slow me down and there's nothing I can do about it. I believe things happen for a reason.

Two years ago I had gotten off work early around 3:30 p.m. I could run about ten errands before picking up Jordan at daycare by 6:00 p.m. I was on my fifth errand and it was going pretty well until I got stuck in traffic. I was trying to catch the credit union open, and in my haste, I did a really fast U-turn on a red light. Well, because of what happened next, I should have just waited at the red light!

As made the U-turn, my tire was punctured by a nail. I felt that something was wrong. There was nothing I could do but call AAA to come and fix my tire (because of this incident, I now know how to fix my own tire!) It took AAA one hour and 45 minutes to arrive. So, I thought to myself, I need to slow down, relax and call someone to pick up my son, as it was 5:40 p.m.

Daycare is very serious about deadlines. Every five minutes late is $5, but that wasn't it. I was late one time because of a meeting, and I called to let them know but I felt like an awful mom. When I got there and saw Jordan's face, it was as though he was saying, "Like mom, what's up...why am I not as important as that meeting?" Now he was 11 months at the time, and couldn't talk, but his face was really saying all that. I felt guilty. So I thought of all my meetings and demands. Well, because I had to wait for AAA, I had time to reflect on my life. I must say that the first 20 minutes I couldn't relax because I had things to do, but I had no choice. So, I slowed down.

It happened about a couple of years ago but that lesson is very valuable to us as single mothers. We are always trying to do it all. Simply, slow down and it will get done. For those things that don't get done, just relax and do the best you can.

22
SINGLE WORKING INGENUIOUS MAMA

I believe that the Single Working Ingenuious Mama (S.W.I.M.) is a blessing from God. The determination, tenacity and persistence to strive against all odds and excel and makes us special.

When I think of us S.W.I.M., there are a great number of titles we juggle everyday. We are also daughters, counselors, sisters, teachers, friends, co-workers, girlfriends, etc. African American single mamas are "sheroes"
    My definition of a Shero is a woman who does the extraordinary with just the ordinary. When thinking about us working mothers, we have two full-time jobs. One is working inside the home and the other is working outside the home to provide for the families. A couple of suggestions to maintain a positive attitude as a single working mother are:

1. Learn to delegate, it's okay to ask for help.
2. When you feel overwhelmed with a situation, walk away and come back later with a clear head.
3. Don't be so hard on yourself! Do the best you can do. So many times we look back and say if only we would have done it this way, oh well. Let it go and move on!
4. Give yourself credit for making the choice to be a single mother.
5. Be proud to be a single African American mother.
6. There will be a lot of balls in the air while juggling everything, and it's okay to let a couple fall on to the floor. Just remember to pick them up. Think of a better way to juggle or ask someone to help.

23
PUSH ME AND I'LL FLY
(Role Models: They Are
The Wind Beneath My Wings)

I'm blessed to see positive striving sisters who have made a difference in my world. I believe that seeing African American women who are national talk show hosts, civil right activists, poets, editors-in-chief, presidents of Black universities, best-selling authors, a physically challenged, successful congresswoman and successful single mothers have played an important role in my life. The positive African American women I speak of are: Barbara Jordan, Iyanla Vanzant, Rosa Parks, Oprah Winfrey, Susan L. Taylor, my mother - Helen Williamson, Teresa McFadden, Maria Dowd, Johnetta Cole, Maya Angelou, Julia Boyd, BeBe Moore Campbell and a host of other sister friends.

To all of you I say <u>thank you</u> for empowering me! At one time or another, you have encouraged, motivated, inspired and enriched my life. As I stated earlier, a person can't be what a person can't see. Seeing these dynamic sisters in action, has made me believe I indeed can fly.

24
THANK YOU

It is very important to acknowledge our gratitude to others by one little word when you put them together – Thank you. It's such a small word for large, generous things that people do. Sometimes we think people should do things for us and we forget to say thank you. It's important to acknowledge when people do good things for us and let them know we appreciate it by saying thank you. Here are other suggestions of how to thank a person:

1. A thank you note expressing your appreciation for their generosity.
2. The telephone is my way to reach out to a friend far away and thank them for being there.

When people feel appreciated, they feel valued. Everyone is special. So the next time someone does something for you no matter how small, say thank you and watch their response. Appreciation is appreciated!

25
GIVE BACK TO THOSE YOU LOVE

We are always taking from those we love, however, we become more fulfilled by giving back.

My father had a stroke in 1994 on the left side of his body and he's regaining the use of his left side slowly through physical therapy. He needs help. He's always hurting and he can't do for himself what he use to. My mother has been excellent with him. I thank God for her everyday.

When my dad had the stroke, I was 3000 miles away in California. I was there emotionally when my mother called for support, but felt she needed more than just hearing my supportive voice on the telephone.

I always tell my father I love him and appreciate him for instilling me with great values and integrity. I decided to move back to Detroit to help out my parents. I'm thankful that I can help by giving my mother a break from taking care of my father and letting my father know he is loved. The other day my mother needed me, and it did my heart good to know I was only 10 miles away and would be right over.

As you continue to experience life, ask yourself, "What is really important?" The answer should be family – the people you love and never seem to have enough time for until something devastating happens. I suggest that you begin by prioritizing what is really important in your life. Then ask, "Will this be important in one, five, ten years from now?" Jobs come and go, but loved ones are here to stay.

OBSTACLES BUILD CHARACTER

I often think of my father's favorite saying, "What doesn't kill you makes you stronger." I usually reply, "I must be superwoman because I've had my share of challenges!"

One of my challenges was struggling with the issue of getting a divorce. In my life, I have always set goals, achieved them and went on to the next one. Never on my "dream list" did I imagine getting a divorce. This was a failure in my world.

I thought that there must have been something I could have done to make our marriage work (always the eternal optimist), but there wasn't and I had to face it. The questions I often ask may be helpful to you:

1. Why is this happening to me?
2. What is the lesson being taught?

I believe that everything happens for a reason. I may not welcome the obstacles, but I'm thankful they come along to help me understand life's journey a little better.

27
RAFIKI'S WISDOM

The "Lion King" is one of those movies that Jordan just loves to watch. So we watch this movie often. I was getting a little tired of the movie until I decided to really watch it and gain a fresh perspective.

Rafiki is a wise monkey in Lion King. He hits Simba (the main character who's not sure of what he should do) on the head and then tells him, "You can run from your problem or learn from it." I found this statement to be very wise.

So many times we try to run or avoid our problems. But if we meet our challenges head on, imagine how empowered we will feel about our situation and ourselves. Our confidence will increase because of what we can accomplish when learning from our problems, versus running away from them.

28
INVEST TIME AND INSTILL LOVE INTO YOUR CHILDREN: IN RETURN YOU WILL RECEIVE A LIFETIME OF JOY AND HAPPINESS

Time is a precious commodity if you use it wisely. I love to read and talk to Jordan. I ask how he is doing and what did he do for the day. Questions to evoke conversation and let him know that he is special and I value him in my life. So many times the little things we do have the most impact on our child's life. Here are suggestions:

1. Create quality time for you and your child.
2. Read to your child. If they are exposed early to books, they will develop a greater appreciation for reading.
3. Tell your child you love him/her.
4. Hug your child often.
5. Recognize their achievements.
6. Say thank you.

If you do this regularly just like stock, your investment will yield a great positive return rate giving you a lifetime of joy and happiness.

VISUALIZE YOUR SUCCESS

Have you ever wanted something and hoped that it would just work out. The answer is probably – yes. However, I encourage you to visualize your success and "see" what you want to accomplish. Write down what you want out of life; for example, a new job, a new car, a best-seller, a loving partner, etc.

Let's take a loving partner as an example. What characteristics do you want your man to possess? Here are some examples: sensitive, considerate, artistic, affectionate, warm, imaginative, spiritual, real, loving, intelligent, and a positive male figure in your child's life. Be very specific and have a plan of action about how to get it. Believe that you deserve success and continue to work on your inner self. Keep pumping yourself up! Believe that you are a good catch and a man would be blessed to have you. Watch out, there may be so many men knocking on your door that you don't know what to do with them. The key here, is visualizing your success and believing in yourself. You are worthy of the successes that come into your life.

30
NEVER GIVE UP

There was a 65 year old man who had a recipe that he thought was a good investment. He went to different restaurants asking people to try this new recipe. He received a great deal of rejection. I'm told he received 1009 no's – can you imagine?

When someone tells us no – think how quickly we give up sometimes. So picture if you will 1009 no's –WOW!!!! So instead of this elderly man giving up, he decided to create his own restaurant. The man I'm speaking of is the Colonel of Kentucky Fried Chicken (KFC). This is a true story. Let me assure you that I could easily own stock in the restaurant as much as I visit the place! This is one of my favorite restaurants, and I can't imagine my life without KFC (I LOVE CHICKEN)!

I'm sure that he probably got a little down as we single mothers will do sometimes but he didn't give up. The secret is to pick yourself up and try again. I recommend prayer for I believe prayer changes things. If you get discouraged, look at different options and ask P.L.U.S. for moral support. Most importantly, remember the Colonel Sanders and how he found success through perseverance and belief in his dream.

31
THE GLASS IS HALF FULL
(My Perception)

Your perception – your reality. How much water is in the glass is really how you view the glass itself.

There is a story about identical twins. Who only had one quality that was different from each other. One twin, Larry, was optimistic and his brother John was pessimistic. Larry was put into a room full of manure and John was put into another room with a brand new bicycle and many toys. When they went to check up on John, he was crying complaining that the toys were going to eventually break. When the observers went to check up on Larry, he was throwing manure up in the air. They asked what he was doing, and he replied that with all this manure there had to be a pony in there somewhere.

It's necessary to find the positive in every situation. Three ways to keep the glass half full:

1. Believe that it's full.
2. By thinking positive there will be a positive outcome.
3. Ask yourself the next time a situation happens, where's the positive?

FINANCIAL FITNESS PLAN

When I hear the word budget, I immediately think that I'm being deprived, I don't like being deprived so I have to play word games with myself. These words are positive and help with the Successful Financial Fitness Plan. There are seven strategies I use to keep me on the right track:

1. Reduce the cost of luxuries. Instead of spending money on fast food, create a home cook meal such as; Spaghetti. This meal would cost under $4.00 and feeds a family of six, instead of going to an expensive salon try a Beauty College and save 35%.

2. Change your attitude. Just like losing weight won't work if you focus on how much you eat, financial fitness won't work if you focus on how much you can spend before plunging into debt.

3. Avoid temptation and places that tempt you to spend money.

4. Simplify your life – cut up all but one credit card. Consolidate all prior debts. Pay your credit cards off or have an aggressive time line for paying them off.

5. Reward yourself. It's much easier to stick to a lifestyle plan if you can look forward to something special each time you reach a short term goal. For example, after saving $250 treat yourself to a play or book (whatever brings you pleasure) and this will also encourage success.

6. Surround yourself with supportive friends and family members who encourage you to succeed.

7. Take a break - Everyone needs a break once in a while. You've been really good and then you see this blouse and you really want it buy it. It's important to be disciplined but it's also necessary to not feel deprived.

This strategy often causes a lot of stress for single mothers because of the lack of money in your budget. Sometimes expenses outweigh the monthly income that you are taking home. I suggest to be aware of what you spend your money on. Most of all, question if you really need that item.

33
MAXIMIZE YOUR LIFESTYLE

As single mothers, if we treasure ourselves and get the most out of life, we will enhance our personal growth. The way to make this happen is to create the following:

1. Balance in the area of finance. Develop a spending plan that will suit your income.
2. Eat nutritiously. Healthy food that will enhance your lifestyle.
3. Exercise to fit your lifestyle at least three times a week for 30 minutes.
4. Allow quality time for yourself. The time that you give to yourself will allow a more positive lifestyle.

Let's take this a step further by investing in ourselves. If you feel good about yourself, you will also share that goodness with your child.

34.
PUT HUMOR IN YOUR LIFE

Learn to laugh at yourself. Life is just too precious to go through it so uptight and seriously. We will miss some of life's most valuable lessons if we don't take time to lighten up.

I used to work in a very high stress job and I would put out about ten fires a day (sticky situations to fix). Someone would come into my office and say, "I hate my job." Normally my response would be sarcastic and somewhat drastic so the person could see themselves and laugh. I would say, "Could you be a little more negative, so I can really understand. What's so bad?"

I encourage you to find humor in life. When Jordan was about six months old and I would change his diaper, he would "pee" at the moment I was changing him and soak the nice outfit I just put on him. I remember looking at Jordan and laughing, because it wasn't like he planned it. We just have to go with the flow, so to speak.

35

IT DOESN'T COST ANYTHING
TO SHOW KINDNESS TO OTHERS,
BUT IT MEANS A GREAT DEAL

I have noticed among our sister friends that it doesn't cost us anything to show kindness through a compliment, encouraging word or a listening ear. We are not in this world alone we need each other. However, it is disturbing to me the number of sisters who, for no apparent reason, appear to have a chip on their shoulders. They don't want to say "hi" or look at you, as if you have a problem when you smile at them. The next time you have an opportunity to be kind, don't let it slip away. You may be lifting someone's spirit and you don't even realize how important such a small act is really is to her.

It would be remarkable if we, as African American women, would help each other unconditionally. The next time you see a sister friend say <u>hello</u> and ask how she is doing and listen to the response. One of the sayings I value is: You get more with honey than you can get with vinegar. You may not like bees, but recognize how much more enjoyable your relationships with sister friends could be in the months and years ahead.

36
THE SOUL FOOD CONNECTION

After seeing "Soul Food," I began to ponder why African American families don't take enough time to connect with each other until there's a death or an emergency.

I challenge you to connect with family members weekly or bi-weekly. You never know what tomorrow may bring; a loved one can be here today and gone next week.

When at my cousin's funeral last week, I was confident that I had told him how much I valued him before he died. So live life to its fullest, show love to those you love and in return, you will receive love. Family is precious, so let's treat each with a great deal of love.

37
CHALLENGES PROVIDE
OPPORTUNITY FOR GROWTH

As a very positive person one of my biggest challenges was working with very negative and critical staff members. It was not an easy task to handle. In my previous position in California, we had a staff meeting every Tuesday, and I absolutely dreaded this day. I loved my job but just couldn't understand how everything was wrong. Why those things that I felt were workable were unacceptable to our staff.

What this challenge provided was to be more assertive and ask these questions:

1. What is really going on?
2. What can we do as a team, to work through this issue?

I have always enjoyed harmony. What I learned, however, is that conflict is a necessary tool in order to get to the root of the problem. So when you face a challenge, ask yourself the question:
"What is the opportunity for growth in this situation?"

38
STOP WHINING AND SEEK
A POSITIVE OUTCOME

Have you ever noticed how easy it is to complain rather than see the positive? Matt B. Rees is a very special brother I worked with who believes that if you don't like a situation or the way you look, you should do something about it. He's a very positive self-confident brother who doesn't have much tolerance for people who just whine and do nothing to change their plight. Matt believes that's wasted energy and I agree with him. Suggestions that would help here are:

1. Give yourself 24 hours to whine. After that create a plan of action to come up with a positive solution.
2. Ask yourself why am I constantly whining? To get attention, which is (mostly negative). Or do people just expect me to whine. If you would take a survey, most people could do without whining.

39
SELF EMPOWERMENT

I enjoy the saying, "Give a person a fish and she will eat for a day. Teach a person how to fish and she can eat for a lifetime". If you say this in the presence of Kelly Ann Elizabeth Marie Boland, an artist and a very valuable employee. She would look around and say "I don't even like fish that much." I supervised Kelly for a year and saw her blossom just like a rose. She has gifts that still amaze me when I see her in action. One thing Kelly and I disagreed on is her ability. Kelly didn't have the confidence to execute different events, I put her in situations that enabled her to see how spectacular and successfully she could do the job. After a long discussion of why I believed that she could do it, I empowered Kelly to be better than she ever imagined.

As single mothers, we must enable ourselves to go beyond our comfort zone and push ourselves in areas that we would never attempt. For example, if you haven't received that G.E.D. and believe it won't make any difference, try thinking it will. Ask how can I enable myself to be more than I ever thought I could be? After you empower yourself, you have the courage to empower your child. When children start achieving their goals, they develop confidence, and begin to believe they are capable of doing anything for the sky is the limit.

40
BE BLESSED, NOT STRESSED

Ten ways to reduce stress from your average day:

1. Begin and end your day with prayer.
2. Wake up thirty minutes early.
3. Map out your day so you can control your time, and not let time control you.
4. Ask for help from friends and family members.
5. Fit exercise into your day.
6. Don't work on your lunch break. Do something you enjoy that's all about you!
7. Call a P.L.U.S. friend just to say "hi"and you'll feel better.
8. Eat regular, nutritious meals.
9. Simplify your life. It's easier than you think. When you come home and the phone rings and you don't want to answer it, let it go to voice mail.
10. Take a P.M.V. (Positive Mental Vacation) before starting dinner.

41
TREAT YOURSELF LIKE YOUR BEST FRIEND

Sherry Lynn Kelly is a communications specialist and professor from Detroit whom I have known for almost 25 years. She is my very best friend and Jordan's Godmother. Sherry loves the arts and culture, such as theaters, museums and concerts. We hang out and have quality dinners, go to church, discuss the ups and downs of relationships, and encourage each other to shed those unwanted pounds or sometimes just laugh at ourselves. Although she complains about my suggestions on life, I'm amazed at how much she values them. Sherry has been instrumental in the typing and the retyping of this book.

Before I became a mother, Sherry and I always hung out together, so it was quite an adjustment for her when I returned home and devoted most of my time to Jordan and my family. Although she is a terrific person, Sherry's patience can be somewhat short. She used to teased me and say that she would "divorce" me because we still hardly see each other since I returned to Detroit.

Well, I really enjoy my time with a good book watching the latest Disney movie, singing nursery rhymes to Jordan and going to bed early. However, Sherry loves to hang out. I still try to make her part of my world, and she in turn has become more patient and understanding. I guess that's why we remain best friends.

Just as I try to sacrifice time for Sherry, what things would you do for your best friend that you could do for yourself? Make a conscious effort to be as good to yourself as you would for your best friend.

42
CAN DO SPIRIT

"If you think you can or if you think you can't, you're right."
– Henry Ford

This is a line that Sharon R.Willey, a colleague and a friend would say at least twice a day. I supervised Sharon for about two years, and can't remember her ever telling me that she couldn't do something. I believe that's why she is still a P.L.U.S. in my life because like Sharon, I believe if you can you will get what you think you can. I believe that there's no such word as can't. If you erase the apostrophe and the "t," you have "can." If you think you can, then you can. I believe that if you reach for the moon even if you miss, you'll be among the stars. One of my friends always teases me about getting poked from a star. I respond to him by saying that it is good to make the attempt. It is better to have tried and failed, than to have not ever tried.

I always hear from friends and co-workers "You can't be this positive, it's annoying!" I have a lot of reasons and situations that have happened in my life where I could be negative. But like everything in my life, I push myself to strive for excellence in all areas. The best in you will come out if you have a "can do" spirit. People gravitate toward you and it will just ooze out all around you. I'm especially partial to the word "spirit" because it represents our soul and courage.

Children can't be what they can't see. If they see their mama having a "can do" spirit, then maybe they too, will think it's possible.

43
YOU ARE MY SUNSHINE
(Positive Daily Message)

"You are my sunshine, my only sunshine. You make me happy when skies are gray, Jordan. You'll never know Jordan, how much I love you, please don't take my sunshine away, Jordan." Every morning since he was about two months old I have sung this to him. I'm not a singer, but Jordan doesn't seem to mind. He doesn't like getting up in the mornings, but when I sing this song adding Jordan's name whenever I feel like it, he begins to smile and starts singing along.

The other day, I overslept and Jordan was sitting next to me singing "You Are My Sunshine." First I was excited that he woke me up in time. After I took my shower, I realized a very valuable lesson. Jordan is my son and my student. Whatever I want him to learn, I can instill that in him now. Well, he spent the night over at my mother's house and guess what? He woke up singing that song. It confirmed that I have to be careful of everything I do as a parent because he is watching me closely and is picking up every thing I say and do. Here are suggestions:

1. Reinforce that your child is your sunshine.
2. When your child does small or large things, accentuate the positive.

44
IN SPITE OF ALL, GOD IS GOOD

If you call my parent's house and my mother answers the phone, she will greet you by saying: "Inspite of all, God is good." When I was younger, this used to irritate me because I didn't understand the real meaning of this phrase. As I matured, I have really come to believe and value this statement.

I remember having a challenging day in California, it was around 3:30 a.m. and 6:30 a.m. my mom's time, and I just wanted to talk through my situation and really get her perspective. When she answered the phone and said "In spite of all God is good," I began to cry immediately and really reflect on that phrase. This is because in the midst of my challenging crisis I forgot, "In spite of all God is good!"

As single mothers, we will experience a few valleys during our journey, just remember and never forget that, "In spite of all, God is good."

45
THE A.T.M. PERSPECTIVE

When you interact with people on a daily basis do you consider them a deposit or a withdrawal? Do you add to the quality of someone's day – deposit? Or do you take from the person – withdrawal? Strive to make a deposit to the people with whom you come in contact with everyday. If you say something positive, watch how much you give back to that individual. On the flip side, if you don't have something nice to say, try giving constructive criticism focusing on the behavior and not the individual. I especially like the A.T.M. perspective because so many of us use the A.T.M., because it is quicker. However, remember that just as quickly as you can withdraw, you can deposit.

Our challenge for the rest of life's journey is to be mindful of making human deposits. What positive messages do you give to others? Think of human withdrawals – how many negative messages you give to others. So many times as mothers we are not even aware of how fast we can impact our children with withdrawals and deposits. Take a deep breath and count to ten before connecting with your child if it's going to be a withdrawal. Try to make as many deposits as you possibly can. There are going to be times where you have to withdraw but see how you can turn those into deposits.

46
I'M DOING JUST FINE

So many times we are perceived as unhappy, single women who need a man to take care of us. This is a myth. The Boys II Men song, "Doin' Just Fine," expresses the sentiments that made me say, "Yeah, I'm doing just fine!!!" As single mothers we should strive to be happy and put the energy into ourselves and our child. If some special man comes along that's great, but if he doesn't we can still be just fine on our own. We just have to believe that we are a Nubian Queen, and that's how we should be treated by our mate.

I suggest you evaluate what you want in a mate and rethink your values. If you're sad or depressed or just want someone to hold on to, call up a P.L.U.S. to help you through this valley and you'll be on your way to doing just fine.

THE JOURNEY IS AS IMPORTANT AS THE DESTINATION

So many times when we are taking a trip, we are so focused on getting to our destination that we overlook the journey. I attended a play called, "Why Do Good Girls Like Bad Boys," and one of the actors said, "When we are going through the journey and it's difficult, it appears that there's no way out. God wouldn't bring us this far not to see us through it." That just struck a chord with me. We as single mothers have our share of disappointments, challenges and valleys, but always remember that God wouldn't give us more than we can bear. I urge you to really look at the journey and see what you could acquire as you reach your destination.

48
KEEP YOUR HEAD UP

When I think of this saying, Keep Your Head Up. I want you to feel encouraged throughout life's journey.

Here are the Top 10 strategies to help you establish and maintain a positive attitude:

1. Take a Positive Mental Vacation (P.M.V.) everyday. It's an inventory of what's going on that's positive in your life.
2. Maximize Your Lifestyle! Create a balance in the area of finance, nutrition, exercise and quality time for yourself.
3. Shift your way of thinking.
4. Look at the mirror two ways. How you see yourself in the mirror and how you feel about yourself (Self-esteem).
5. Remember to S.E.E. the good – establish (Self Esteem Enhancers)
6. Create and maintain P.L.U.S. (Positive Loving Understanding Supporters) in your life.
7. Run at an exceptionally high speed to avoid N.A.G.S. (Negative Annoying Gloomy Supporters).
8. Show me some love. Hug your child daily.
9. Lighten up! Go with the G.L.O.W. (God's Light will provide Opportunity for a Winning attitude). Be blessed, not stressed.
10. Believe you can fly. Nourish your dreams.

I want to leave you with this thought: When in doubt, be strong. We have a choice, so choose to be strong and *Keep Your Head Up.*

Dear Sister Friend:

*I hope in this book motivated, encouraged and in-
spired you to "Keep Your Head Up."*

*In the spirit of sisters helping sisters, I would love to
hear from you about the wisdom, motivation, or
motto that encouraged you to "Keep Your Head Up"
when it was a challenge in your life.*

*I look forward to hearing from you, and thanks for
purchasing the book!*

Please send correspondence to:

Thomastine W. Ureh
P.O. Box 1353-I
Lincoln Park, MI 48146

Treasure Yourself,

Thomastine